How to Pray:
Living Wholly Through Honest, Surrendered, Heart Praying

How to Pray
Living Wholly Through Honest, Surrendered, Heart Praying

The Book
Strengthen your intimate connection with God by journeying to honest, surrendered, heart praying.
978-0-9967655-0-3

The Study Guide
This study guide, based on the book, *How to Pray*, is suitable for both individuals and groups.
978-0-9967655-1-0

The Devotional
28 days of devotions with journal pages on themes from the book, *How to Pray*.
978-0-9967655-2-7

The CD
28 audio reflections on themes from the book, *How to Pray*, that guide you to go deeper and make the book more personal.
978-0-9967655-3-4

For more information, visit:
http://surrenderinprayer.com/how-to-pray

HOW TO PRAY

Living Wholly Through Honest, Surrendered, Heart Praying

Claire Annelise Smith

SurrenderInPrayer Press
Mission, KS

HOW TO PRAY:
LIVING WHOLLY THROUGH HONEST, SURRENDERED, HEART PRAYING

Copyright © 2015 by Claire Annelise Smith

All rights reserved. No part of this book may be reproduced or transmitted in any form or by any means without written permission from the author.

ISBN 978-0-9967655-0-3

All Scripture quotations are from New Revised Standard Version Bible, copyright © 1989 National Council of the Churches of Christ in the United States of America. Used by permission. All rights reserved.

Cover photo: David M. Schrader/123rf.com
Author photo: Isaac Alongi

Printed in the United States of America by SurrenderInPrayer Press

To all seekers:

"Then when you call upon me and come and pray to me, I will hear you. When you search for me, you will find me; if you seek me with all your heart," Jeremiah 29:12-13.

Acknowledgment

God is good, and I give God thanks for guiding me in this endeavor. I am blessed to be surrounded by people who care and have supported me in writing *How to Pray: Living Wholly Through Honest Surrendered, Heart Praying.* A special thank you to Bill, Gay, Kathy, Marilyn, Oleta, my siblings, and Old Mission UMC. This book could not have been completed without you.

Contents

Introduction

It Doesn't Have to Be This Way. 1

Chapter One

Missing You. 3

Chapter Two

Missing God. 20

Chapter Three

Missing Prayers. 34

Chapter Four

Living Wholly. 55

Introduction

It Doesn't Have to Be This Way

How do you pray when everything around you seems disjointed and you feel fragmented? How do you pray when your life is filled with stress?

Something's missing. You sense it. Even though you can't put your finger on it, you want it—a life that feels complete. You say to yourself: "Life should not be this stressful and fragmented. Where is a clear sense of direction? Whatever became of clarity and peace?" Something's missing. The parts are not holding together.

When you pray, your prayers often ring hollow. It's as if you've come to bake a cake. All of the ingredients are there. However, none is in the right quantity. Thus, you're missing parts. The cake is not holding together.

Yet, you can recover the missing parts. You can feel complete and learn to pray in a fuller way.

You see, to live with greater clarity and peace in this world, you need to know how to pray so that you experience God more fully through honest, surrendered heart praying. Experiencing God more fully allows you to live an integrated life that is complete.

When you approach God with honest, surrendered, heart praying, you will go to God on God's terms. You will go past the God of your imagination to the God as revealed in the Bible. This is your road to greater clarity and peace.

How to Pray

There are four chapters in this book. Chapter One, "Missing You," looks at ways in which we miss ourselves through fear, a lack of knowledge and, building on the wrong foundations for security. Chapter Two, "Missing God," invites us to take another look at how we see, understand, and therefore relate to God. Chapter Three, "Missing Prayers," examines the effect that missing God and ourselves has on our prayers as well as the ways in which our prayers are often limited in depth and reach. Chapter Four, "Living Wholly," picks up on the previous chapters and goes more deeply into how to pray by starting with God, dealing with ourselves, and engaging in real praying.

These four chapters are a whole. They teach you how to pray by exposing the missing parts that need to be held together. Then, they give you clear direction on what it means to offer honest, surrendered, heart praying. In this way you will live the full life of clarity and peace that you desire and for which you have been created.

The chapters use anecdotes to make the points real. These anecdotes illustrate all the key points. They are based on situations that the author has encountered in various stages of her ministry and life. The names have all been changed.

This book is written from a Christian perspective. However, all are invited to share so that you know how to pray to experience God more fully and live wholly with greater clarity and peace.

Chapter One

Missing You

Emily tried very hard to avoid looking into the mirror. She was afraid of what she would see. When she was young, her mother had tried to tell her that she was beautiful. She had a hard time believing it. After all, mom was biased. Truth be told, Emily still had a hard time believing it. It seemed as if people gave her strange looks when she went to the grocery store and other places.

Whenever she was at the checkout counter, Emily looked at the magazines. At home, she viewed a lot of television shows and she was discouraged by what she saw as she looked at the celebrities. She just knew that she was not pretty enough, not thin enough, not vivacious enough, not . . . enough.

Is that you? Well, maybe not. However, we can get in the way of us going to God with honest, surrendered, whole hearted praying. When you are missing you, what are you taking to God in prayer? While you may not be as insecure as Emily, the truth is many of us are not sure that we measure up.

Fear

Many of us are going around with a hidden fear of not being good enough. Sometimes it's at the conscious level. Very often, it's at the subconscious level. What feeds it?

How to Pray

There are three main elements that feed this fear: (1) Things that have been said to us and/or actions that were designed to put us down and make us feel less than acceptable, (2) comparing ourselves with others, and (3) using the wrong filters.

The Put Down

It's funny how one remark can affect us for good or for ill. It can leave an indelible impression on us. For some reason, as human beings we tend to be more affected by negative than by positive comments. We remember them more. Thus, the put down is a bruising blow to the soul that can have long term consequences. This is what happened with Sebastian.

Sebastian felt as if he'd been sucker punched. It was as if the air had been sucked out of him after hearing a trusted adult say that he was not the brightest lamp in the harbor. Years later, Sebastian still doubted himself. He pushed himself to excel. Each time he received a grade that was on the lower end of the scale he relived the pain and inadequacy of those early comments.

Are you like Sebastian, maybe just a little? Perhaps it was something that you overheard, like, "He'll/She'll never amount to much." Possibly, it was something that was said to your face such as, "You look terrible," when you had taken extra care with your appearance. It could have been a snub from someone who was important to you. Regardless of the source, it left a mark on you that feeds your fear of not being good enough.

As a result, we miss the God-given gifts and strengths that we have. We doubt that we have those gifts, even when other people affirm them. The wrong script plays in our heads, the one created by insensitive comments. Therefore, we stay in the "safe zone," afraid to try new things. When we pray, we're not open to hearing all that God says to us and all the places to which God would lead us. The wrong script keeps pushing that away. We're missing all that God can do in and through us. We're missing who we are.

Moreover, when we pray we are not fully open to God. We have transferred the fear of not being good enough to God. We harbor a secret fear that God will put us down. As a result, we keep a part of ourselves locked away from God to protect us from a put down from God. This leads us to another missing piece in our praying—the comparison.

The Comparison

How do you feel when you are on the receiving end of being compared with another person? That probably depends on whether or not you come out in a positive light. While it seems second nature to compare, it's not fun when people compare us with others, implying that the other person is better than we are. Do you know what's worse? When we compare ourselves with others in an unfavorable way. That's what happened to Elizabeth. It affected her life and her praying.

Elizabeth looked at Anna and sighed. Anna seemed to have it all: looks, figure, popularity. If only she was more like Anna she would get a better job. Angrily, she asked God why God hadn't made her like Anna.

From high school to college into adult life, Elizabeth had compared herself with others. She always did this to her own detriment because somehow in her comparing, she was always less than those around her.

Elizabeth became more and more discontented with her appearance and life. She sighed deeply. She would never be good enough. She continually asked God to change her appearance.

One day, Elizabeth had an epiphany. God loved her as she was. She stopped comparing herself with others and her prayers changed.

Have you ever been Elizabeth? You look around you and you see people that you consider to be very beautiful and/or handsome and intelligent. You decide that you could never be like them. Coupled with this, you look at the media and/or your friends' social media feed. Everyone seems happy and on the move into the good life. Once again, you decide that you could never be like them. You feel inadequate.

To compensate, we subconsciously look for people that we consider to be inferior to us. We may even seek out shows that star such people. Ah. Now we have some people whom we're above. We've made it.

Whether or not you know it, you've given in to the fear of not being good enough each time you compare yourself with others. You've missed the point and you've missed you.

You are uniquely and wonderfully made by a loving Creator. Of course, there'll always be room for improvement, but you are fantastically and irreplaceably you, as you are. No one can be you. No one else can make the contributions you have been put on earth to make. Don't allow comparisons to keep you from fully presenting all of yourself to God and asking God to show

Missing You

you what God has in store. This leads us to the issue of using the wrong filters.

The Wrong Filters

There's nothing wrong with admiring others and aspiring to emulate some of their qualities. We're missing who we are as God's unique people when we seek to be completely like others or compare ourselves with them. When we aspire to be like them, we're using the wrong filters. Here's an example.

Mia had great aspirations. They consumed her prayers for she'd always been taught to pray to God about all her concerns. Her prayers focused on being successful. "Dear God, let me be successful like . . . ." She never once paused to consider what God might want her to do, much less ask God about it. It never crossed her mind to define success in terms of living out the values of God's kingdom. Mia's models of success were lifted from the pages of magazines and news stories without applying any filters.

What filters could Mia have used? For starters, when she saw people that she admired, she could have asked herself: Is this person seeking to glorify God in all that she or he does and says? Does this person give more than a passing nod to prayer? That's what you can do as well.

Next, check to see if the attitudes and actions of your models of success line up with the greatest commandments of loving God and loving neighbors. Who are these neighbors? Other people who also inhabit the earth. Additionally, check to see the level of respect the people you admire show for God's created order.

The big thing though, is that Mia had not developed confidence in who God had made her to be. If she had, she would have started by praying into her God-given uniqueness. Then she would have looked at others more as a reference.

There'll always be people that we admire. However, if like Mia, we do so from a place of fear and insecurity, defining success and who we want to be will be on their terms. The filters we use will shift us from putting a priority on living out of love for and to the glory of God. Therefore, before we emulate any aspect of another's life let's look for commitment to God and qualities that are in keeping with God's values. That's what we can ask God to make real in our lives. We do so as we follow Jesus Christ, all the while focusing more on living and praying into our uniqueness.

Lack of Self-Awareness

How well do you know you? If any of the above sections is true, it's evident that we're missing a part of who we are. As we've seen fear can keep us from knowing and embracing ourselves. However, there's another aspect to missing you that goes beyond the fear of not being good enough. We may have embraced our God-given gifts and strengths but still be lacking in self-knowledge.

It's important that we understand and value who we truly are, why we do what we do, and how we feel. Yet, knowing ourselves is not as simple as it sounds. We are complex people made up of our past and present, including our many interactions with others. We are continually evolving. Moreover, we carry

Missing You

blind spots, regardless of our age. Thus, we need to be open to the ways in which God will use situations and people to give us deeper insight into ourselves.

Hidden Wounds

So often we carry scars and wounds of which we are unaware. In the moment, we suppress them so that we can keep carrying on. Yet, they remain to trip us up when we least expect it. They are often below the surface. Pausing to examine what we do and why would help us to recognize the signs of unresolved conflicts and wounds. Then we would be better able to go below the surface and open up hitherto unknown parts to God for healing. This is what happened with Tommy.

Tommy got into Abe's face. He was mad as all get out. How dare Abe try to correct Tommy. Abe knew nothing about playing the trumpet. Tommy was so mad that he missed the fact that while Abe did not know about playing the trumpet per se, Abe was a well-rounded musician with an ear for what worked well and what didn't.

Tommy's reaction to Abe came from his insecurity. He was very insecure and it showed in how he handled feedback. He did not deal well with criticism of any kind. Inside, he got tied up in knots. Outside, he became very belligerent when others tried to correct him. It was affecting his relationship with others. It was affecting his work. Tommy had a problem.

Abe got real quiet. He didn't say anything. However, the look on Abe's face bothered Tommy. Abe looked as if someone had bushwhacked him. Tommy wanted to cry. "Why do I keep

How to Pray

hurting people," he asked himself? "Dear God, what is wrong with me?" he prayed sincerely.

That night, when Tommy lay in bed he kept praying about it, turning it over in his mind. He thought, "The least I can do is apologize to poor Abe." He did that the next day. That night he prayed again. He was afraid that he would blow up again when he least expected it.

Tommy started going back over his life. He went back as far as when he was in elementary school and realized that's when things changed. There was a lot of stress at home and tempers were short. Everything he did was wrong. He was punished for the simplest things. There was always yelling and screaming. He was afraid to go home, some days. His work and behavior at school were affected. There, he became the butt of ridicule. As the memories came flooding back, he relived the pain of those years.

Tommy was at a crossroads and he knew it. He could suppress the emotions and memories again and allow them to continue affecting his behavior, or he could deal with them, as painful as it would be. He opted for the latter. He prayed again and thanked God for showing him what was wrong. He gave it over to God. Next, he started attending counseling. He undergirded the process with prayer.

Our past is our present whether we like it or not. With ongoing honest, surrendered, heart praying we can uncover the wounds and scars that hold us back and get the help we need as we learn more about ourselves. Moreover, God has placed us in community and we grow through our interactions with each other. Sometimes these interactions are positive. Sometimes, they are negative. Through them we see ourselves more clearly, as in Tommy's case. In addition, through them we are always unfolding.

The Unfolding You

Do you realize that there are aspects of you waiting to be discovered? Some of these you may stumble upon on your own. Others will happen because someone challenged you. Maybe you have already experienced it.

It's true. We can settle into a well-established routine, following familiar patterns, comfortable with the strengths and gifts that we know ourselves to have. However, there is more to us. God will often use people and situations, to bring these out. Let's see how this worked out for Jenny.

Aria asked Jenny to give a speech at the recognition ceremony. This was a new activity for Jenny. However, she didn't want to disappoint Aria. She got help and buckled down to prepare. The big day arrived. Jenny nailed it. She was a natural. Suddenly, she discovered that she was a gifted speaker. The new circumstance allowed a hidden part of Jenny to come to the fore.

Unfolding knowledge of our strengths and gifts is an ongoing part of life's journey. If we decide that we know all that we have to offer and stop there, we'll miss important parts of who we are and who we could become.

It behooves us, therefore, to be open to God revealing previously hidden parts of ourselves in direct and indirect ways. This includes being open to those who may see something in us of which we are unaware.

How to Pray

It could be as simple as someone pointing out to us a strength or something we need to work on that we hadn't even noticed. Has that ever happened to you?

Let's go back to Aria and Jenny. Aria who had asked Jenny to give the speech may have seen the potential in her. Jenny's openness to try something new allowed a strength of hers to flex and grow.

It's a wonderful thing to have something "new" to offer to God and God's people. As we continually evolve, more of our abilities will unfold. Sometimes we and those around us will be surprised. Moving toward greater knowledge of these capabilities allows us to bring more aspects of ourselves into God's light. In God's light we experience greater transformation, all are uplifted, and God is glorified. In turn, we live more wholly.

The Importance of Being With Others

It follows, therefore, that we need to be with others. God has placed us among people. Sure. When we look around we see many imperfections. These imperfections may be among the people in our families, our communities, our churches, and other places. However, if we were to avoid people because of their imperfections, real and imagined, we would miss out big time. Actually, we'd have to avoid people all together. The reality of life is that we're all frail and in need of each other and God's grace.

None of us is perfect. Jesus didn't come and die because the world is perfect. More importantly, though, if we avoided those we deem imperfect we'd be missing the opportunity to grow in self-awareness and we'd be missing parts of ourselves. We grow in self-knowledge as we interact with others. This is what happened to Daniel.

Daniel had a short temper. He had been like that for as long as he could remember. It seemed to him that people were just dumb. He had no patience with dumb and stupid. He was always angry and short-tempered with those around him. When he couldn't express it at work, he stifled it and became more irritable with his children and those with whom he could let down his guard. His wife told him to pray about his temper. He wouldn't. In his head, he didn't have a problem.

One day, she gave him example after example of his impatient attitude towards others and the times when he lost his temper. She repeated the things that he constantly said about others. Daniel could no longer ignore it and decided to follow her advice and pray about it. While he was at it, he prayed about his attitude to others. Daniel gained self-knowledge because the real Daniel showed when he was with others. He also gained greater self-awareness because someone in his circle was honest with him. Now, he could go to God with greater honesty.

Yes. As we interact with others, various aspects of ourselves come out. We grow when we get honest feedback and we receive it.

There are other times when the growth to self-awareness happens through sharing in the joy and/or challenges that others face. As we do this, we find our capacity for caring and empathy enlarged. There are even times when we are surprised at the depth of this capacity. We realize that God has been working on us and we give God thanks.

Then there are those times when we encounter challenging people and situations that draw on and strengthen our inner resources and creativity. For example, we encounter people who are negative toward us and actively work against who we are and what we are seeking to accomplish. The pressure forces us to pray more. When we are able to stand our ground, maintain our composure, and respond with love we grow stronger.

Don't be afraid to interact with other people. Otherwise, you'll miss the opportunity to know yourself better and you'll miss important parts of yourself.

The Quest for Security

Isn't it funny how we can use the same words to mean different things? "Security" seems to be one of those. For some of us it means a job that we will have until retirement. For some people, security is as simple as having a building in which to sleep when the night comes. All these point to the desire for something on which we can count; something that is reliably predictable and ensures our comfort and safety.

The Search for Normalcy

We live in a time of rapid change. We know that change has always been a part of life. It's different now, though. The acceleration of technological development seems to have accelerated the pace of innovation in general. It's as if before you can figure out one thing, it's changed. Take Suzie.

Suzie has worked in communications for a long time. She's always been very competent and delivered good results. Now,

Missing You

she's struggling as she tries to keep up with all the new stuff. She thought that she was doing well with reaching people through the whole Facebook thing, then Instagram came along. Now, she wonders if she'll make it. It's not normal for her anymore. She feels as if she's adrift and missing a part of herself.

Related to these rapid shifts because of technology is the expansion of and to some extent the democratization of information. While major media outlets still control much of the narrative concerning events, issues, and people, other voices are able to tell their stories and get their message out to a wider audience. All of this and more makes some people uncomfortable. Things are not "normal" anymore.

We now have to face issues and situations that were not previously part of our everyday reality. We may find ourselves wishing for a past time when things were "normal." We felt more secure then. We may even find ourselves praying that way. However, is that the way God wants us to pray? Is God stuck in the "normal past?"

It is true that many of us just feel frazzled and out of control. It's as if we're missing a part of ourselves. Hence the wish and the prayers for normal.

It is natural that rapid change would cause us to feel some sense of instability. However, the extent to which it affects our sense of who we are and how whole we feel points to our foundations.

Shaky Foundations

In many ways, this chapter is about foundations. On which foundation are our lives built? Is it on the foundation of being

How to Pray

acceptable to others? Is it on the foundation of values, expectations, and priorities? Is it built on seeking to be like the stars? What about a foundation of partial self-awareness and an avoidance of others and going beneath the surface to greater self-knowledge? Is it built on our sense of normal?

Those are all shaky foundations. They change; sometimes seemingly on a whim. That's why it's important to know and accept the unique person that God says you are; to align yourself with God's values; to keep discovering and growing; to find your security in God and seek guidance to roll with the changes around you. That's what Stefano ultimately did.

Stefano felt as if his heart was squeezing in. It hurt. He had lost everything that he held dear. He had watched as one by one his prized possessions were taken from him. The rug had been pulled from under his feet.

He had not been able to keep up with all the changes at his workplace. God knows he had tried. At the end of the day however, his efforts had not been enough. He had been let go, fired. It hurt. Now, without the money to pay the bills he was in danger of being homeless.

Stefano felt despair. Then he remembered. God was bigger than his situation. He remembered that God did not change even though the circumstances around him changed.

Stefano prayed as he had never done before. Before God he celebrated who he was and faced his weaknesses. He was completely honest with God. His bitterness had become a trap. He gave it and his entire situation over to God. He confessed that he had been building on the wrong foundations, trusting in his successes and accomplishments instead of trusting God. He

Missing You

recommitted himself to God and gave the situation over to God and asked God for direction.

Suddenly, for the first time in months, Stefano felt peace. He followed what God told him to do. The peace came first. The situation did not change overnight, but bit by bit he experienced the turnaround in his situation.

It's easy to rely on our accomplishments and past successes. Though shifting and fleeting, this is what society encourages us to do.

Of course accomplishments and successes are great. We thank God for them and for what they allow us to do. However, they are not stable enough to provide a foundation. They are not stable enough to provide security. That comes from God. This leads us to the importance of space.

Breathing Spaces

It's easy to miss parts of you when you feel as if you don't have the space to breathe. Then you're tempted to take whatever ingredients are at hand to "bake the cake."

Some of you have read this chapter up to this point and think,

"That's all well and good but I can't even think about these things.

"I've been very challenged recently. It seems as if I just run from activity to activity, from helping one person to helping another. My family obligations have me feeling overwhelmed. I'm exhausted at the end of most days. I am so afraid that I am not up to the task and that I will burn out. I'm afraid I'm missing something . . . I'm not sure because I can't think, can't pray. When I think of the future; I try not to think of the future. . . . I badly need a space for myself to think, to pray, to find myself, to breathe, to be at peace again."

Somehow, we feel that if we could just find that space we would have a greater level of security. There is some truth in this. When we have enough space to reconnect with ourselves as it were, we have a greater measure of peace and confidence. However, there is a danger.

There are many people who promise peace. There are many groups who offer the wherewithal to get in touch with your inner person. However, many of them deify the person and not the living God. Thus, the self becomes a circular reference point, the be all and end all of all decisions and arbitrator of right and wrong. This security, therefore, is grounded in feeling rather than in the reality of the love of God seen in Jesus Christ on the cross. It becomes a security of self-fulfillment and self-elevation without accountability to God and our neighbors. Let's look at Molly, a product of this type of group.

Molly felt such tranquility. It amazed even her. She had attended the retreat where she had learned that she was the most important person in the universe and her well-being came first. She didn't have to answer to anyone. She needed to shake off negative people from her life. One of her first tasks when she returned from the retreat, was to tell her sister that she could no longer count on her for support. Parasite! A weight had lifted. She was free.

Ava asked Molly what would happen with Suzie? Couldn't she at least point Suzie to some services that could help her?

Missing You

How would Suzie cope now that she had, without warning, lost the support on which she had counted? Molly said she was not giving up her new-found space for anyone. She had learned how important she was and how to treat herself kindly. No one was going to take that away from her.

Molly's peace was maintained around herself alone and not the commandment to love God and neighbor. It was an insecure breathing space. Any reaching out that stretched her, would shatter her sense of peace and security.

When you inhabit the wrong breathing space, you miss you, for you're missing the you as God created you to be—in community, loving God and neighbor. Of course you are important. Of course, you should take care of yourself.

We can learn from Jesus who knew how to make space for himself. He had times for prayer. He got away when he could. However, he was totally committed to loving and serving God and the people he encountered. He was a man of compassion. We also get a sense of peace about him. There was no striving, except for Gethsemane. Even there, it ended in peace as he submitted to God's will. He was calm and ready.

Thus, we learn from Jesus the importance of breathing space. Such space empowers us to avoid missing ourselves so that we live in love as we experience God more fully.

The resources, centered on prayer, provided in *SurrenderInPrayer* resources empower you to face your situation, establish values and priorities that are in line with God's, find your security in God, and continually bring all that you are before God in honest, surrendered heart prayer and live with greater clarity and peace in this world.

Chapter Two

Missing God

"Hey God," she said. I froze. I cringed inside. "It's God you're talking to," I screamed internally. "It's God. Not your girlfriend. Not your boyfriend." Then I got calmer as my internal monologue continued. "Okay. It's wonderful that she feels comfortable with God and feels free to talk with God anytime. God is real to her" You know that was not the last time, nor the last person I heard address God that way.

Years later, after all the rationalization and telling myself don't be too rigid, "hey God" is still problematic to me.

You see, I can't imagine anyone going up to Queen Elizabeth II and saying, "hey Liz." Even when protocol isn't followed to a T, there's just something about the office. How much more God.

So, in addressing God we seek this balance between the God who is holy and the God who is present and with us. It is the balance between the God we worship and the God who invites us to go to God as a loving parent. Without this balance, we're in danger of missing God. Thus we miss experiencing God more fully through honest, surrendered, heart praying. We miss living with greater clarity and peace in the world.

The Vague God

"There's something out there that's bigger than we are. Let's send some crumbs its way just in case. We don't want to offend and it just might do us some good. In any case, you have to believe in something." That's how many of us view and approach God. While God does not have a shape that we can touch this does not mean that God is vague and without character.

Something-out-there God

Mark was praying really hard. Mark did not know anything about the entity to which he prayed. He just knew that there was a force in the universe that was larger than he was, so he prayed.

Is reaching out to a vague God reserved for people like Mark alone? Not really. Anytime we pray to or serve a God without specific characteristics and identifiable ways of being and doing, we're reaching out to a vague God.

It is true that the God we serve forbids images: "Do not make an idol for yourself—no form whatsoever—of anything in the sky above or on the earth below or in the waters under the earth" (Ex. 20:4). It just cannot be done. God is bigger than anything we can imagine.

Jesus Christ came as God among us. As John tells us: "In the beginning was the Word, and the Word was with God, and the Word was God. . . . And the Word became flesh and lived among us, and we have seen his glory, the glory as of a father's only son, full of grace and truth" (John 1:1, 14). Yet, in his physical, human form Jesus Christ was unlike the infinite, the divine. Thus, we have no physical representation of this boundless God. Hence we are tempted to give in to seeing God as the vague God, the "something-out-there" God. However, in Jesus Christ we see and learn the heart, character, and actions of a God who is real. God is not vague.

When we go to the God who is something-out-there, we miss experiencing God more fully. We're unable to utter honest, surrendered, heart prayers to a vague notion. Think about it. Will you come clean with a vague idea?

Thus, we miss God and the route to clarity and peace. With the something-out-there God, we're just one step away from the just-in-case God.

Just-In-Case God

Have you met the just-in-case God? Lisa has. Lisa is not sure about God. However, she doesn't want to be caught napping. She is doing everything she knows to do that's convenient for her to appease this God, just in case. This just in case God is real: just in case this God is who they say God is, just in case she'll face terrible punishment if she doesn't, just in case . . . . She feels good about serving this just-in-case God.

The just-in-case God is no more tangible than the something-out-there God. The just-in-case God is all about us and our survival. We are not concerned about God at all. As a matter of fact, we're totally missing God. The sad part is that we really don't care as we hedge our bets.

There's no point in getting to know this God intimately. After all, this God may not even exist. This God may simply be a figment of somebody's imagination. Ultimately, this God will

Missing God

not require our whole-hearted devotion. Yes. We're left feeling good but missing God.

Special-Occasions God

We have certain special days and events in the church's calendars. Easter Sunday is one of them. In some places, Christmas Eve is another. For some it's Old Year's Night/New Year's Eve. Typically, churches can expect to see larger numbers of people than usual attending on these occasions. Some of this increase is due to family members visiting. Some of it is due to people "dusting God off" for these special occasions.

Riley is very familiar with the special-occasions God. It's not just that she only goes to church on special occasions. That's the only time she really thinks about God. During the other times, she just goes about her business without much regard for God. She's focused and she's driven by her career as well as preoccupied with family.

The thing is, though, that while on the surface we may be different from Riley, we're really not. For many of us, God is not real enough to be part of our day-to-day lives. Thus, we only call on God at special times. When we opt for the special-occasions God, we're missing experiencing God more fully by choice.

Whether it be the "something out there," "just in time," or the "special occasions' God, they're all vague. These gods lack definition and specificity. They are not gods that you will relate to closely. They are not gods that you will go to in all honesty and full surrender. They will forever remain unknown, to be called up for some sense of immediate need or future security. Thus God remains missing, at worst co-opted.

The Co-opted God

The co-opted God is real. Those who serve this God have gone past the vague God. This co-opted God is in our everyday lives. What distinguishes this god? He is a god of our imagination, our liking, our likeness. We pick the terms and he meets them. Using the Bible, we select aspects of God that appeal to us and ignore the rest.

The Wishy-Washy God.

The human desire for power is strong. We want to know and have control over what's happening. We hate having our choice taken away from us. We have to control some aspects of our environment. Unfortunately, this extends to God. Thus, we seek to command God and tell God how to run our lives and the world. This was the case with Dan.

Dan had his life planned out. He knew exactly what was to happen and when. For his next step he told God his plans, goals and the sequence in which things were to happen. Then, he waited for God to make it happen. After all, as a child of God he was important.

When things went as planned, Dan was happy. When it didn't go as he anticipated, he was angry with God for not following the plan. After all, he, Dan, was important and knew best what his best life should be like.

What a wishy-washy God Dan served! This was a God without power, without knowledge of us and our affairs, without a will. The wishy-washy God is really a caricature of the true and living God.

Missing God

Yet, we often fall into the trap of serving a wishy-washy God. We do so when we fail to acknowledge God's omnipotence, omniscience, and all present state. We fall into the wishy-washy God trap when we forget that our posture before God needs to be humble obedience, for in such the Lord delights: "And all of you must clothe yourselves with humility in your dealings with one another, for 'God opposes the proud, but gives grace to the humble" (1 Pet. 5:5).

We are squarely in this trap when we fail to inquire of the Lord. Or, we can be like the King of Israel and Jehoshaphat—when we inquire and hear what is contrary to our plans we still rush on heedlessly, seeking to coopt God to our agendas, fooling ourselves that we have control over God.[1] I wonder who gets the last laugh. Certainly not us. Still, we persist in this caricature, sometimes going so far as to think that God is just like us.

The Just-Like-Us God

Nora didn't like the people down the road. She thought that they were crude. Of course, God agreed with her. God approved of the people of whom she approved. Her enemies were God's enemies. Her values were God's values. No questions asked.

Have you met Nora? Perhaps you're a little like her. It's not hard to assume that God is just like us. Naturally, we wouldn't say that. Rather, we'd explain all the ways in which God is

---

[1] In 1 Kgs. 22:4-9, 15–18, 29 the King of Israel and King Jehoshaphat inquired of the Lord through the prophet, Micaiah, concerning whether or not they should go into battle. Even though the prophesy indicated a negative outcome they still went into battle and the results were disastrous.

unlike us. Nevertheless, our actions and attitudes show a different story. We don't seek to align ourselves with God's reign and values. Instead, we assume that whatever we think and value God does.

What a waste! Consider who God is. Consider all that God offers. Then see the tragedy in limiting God to being just like us.

No. God is other than we are, as I discuss later in this book. To miss this is to miss experiencing God more fully. A god who is just like you has no authority. Such a god does not elicit honest, surrendered, heart praying, for how could you yield to someone without authority?

Part of the reason we settle for a god just like us goes back to our desire to be in control. Another part, however, has to do with us not engaging in practices that help us to grow in the grace and knowledge of God. Thus, God remains dwarfed in our understanding.

The Superficial God

When we seek to co-opt God we show that we have not availed ourselves of the opportunity to know God more fully. We're settling for the surface.

Now, it's a given that we will never know God completely. God is infinite. We are finite. However, we do have the opportunity to pray in sincerity and study the Bible on our own and with others so that we come to know God more fully. This is what we do in our *SurrenderInPrayer* programs.

Consider the Apostle Paul who gave up everything to know Christ. Paul knew, as Jesus himself said, that it is through Jesus Christ we come to understand God: "All things have been

Missing God

handed over to me by my Father; and no one knows who the Son is except the Father, or who the Father is except the Son and anyone to whom the Son chooses to reveal him" (Luke 10:22). Yet, unlike Paul, we stop at what we learned in Sunday School or what somebody told us. There is no desire to know God deeply and more importantly, to know God on God's own terms. Unfortunately, this superficial engaging with God is prevalent. We see it in Viv.

Viv made a big thing about serving God. She showed up at every event that the church had. She served on as many committees as she could. She got so busy that she missed growing in the knowledge of God.

Viv's knowledge of God was similar to that of a kindergartner. It showed in her praying. Her prayers were very self-centered and intent on manipulating God to do as she wanted. "God is love" for her meant that God loved her and her kind of people. Thus, she had also embraced the wishy washy God. Furthermore, she had co-opted God to be just like her. She couldn't stand anyone who was different and was sure God couldn't either. What was worse, however, is that Viv wanted a superficial God. Viv resisted the thought that there was more to God than she knew. She was very comfortable with her superficial God and did not want to be made uncomfortable. She loved her club aka church, where she tried her hardest to keep out those who would cause her to look more deeply at God and therefore more deeply at herself.

Viv had a certain respect for God, but not enough to take God at God's own terms; not enough to go deep.

It's a sad thing indeed. God offers much, but we settle for little because we want life on our own terms. As a result, we

How to Pray

miss God and all that God offers us. In its place we hold on to our trinkets as we try, without success, to co-opt God. We are left distracted and frazzled, blaming God when we lack clarity and peace. While, all we needed to do was to go to God with our honest, surrendered, heart prayers.

The Irreverent God

In considering the irreverent God, we're taking another look at the issue of balance, aren't we? Jesus demonstrated balance in living before the God who is holy yet approachable. In his dealings with God, especially his praying, Jesus Christ demonstrated love, deep respect, surrender, and therefore obedience. The Bible Study, *Heart Cries: When You Know That God Is All You Need*,[2] takes a look at Jesus' dependence upon God.

For some reason, however, in our age we seem to feel that it is okay to get rid of the reverential approach. Sure we stopped using the term "fear of God" because we didn't want people to be afraid to approach God. We were trying to get away from the concept of God wielding a "big stick" and/or God waiting to zap you every time you did something wrong. Unfortunately, we have developed a "whatever" approach to God. I'm here to break the news: God is way more than "whatever." God is worthy of so much more. Consider Christ's posture before God and there is no justification for the irreverent God.

---

[2]*Heart Cries: When You Know That God Is All You Need* Claire Annelise Smith, 2014, DVD.

Buddy God

Does familiarity really breed contempt? It would seem so. When we get too familiar with someone or something, after a while we stop appreciating and noticing them or it. That's the danger of "hey God." In addition, we'd be hard put to find a basis for it in Scripture.

Were people friends of God? Yes. Were people friends of Jesus Christ? Yes. But always, they stood in awe of God, in awe of Jesus Christ.

In the Scriptures, we find people acknowledging the otherness and superiority of God by bowing down and falling prostrate before God. In addition, they used words to denote God's superiority. They never presumed a familiarity that put either God or Jesus Christ on the same level with them. As I note in the lesson, "Outrageous Otherness," in *Just Praying: Living in the Kingdom of God*,[3] God is and always will be other than we are. Here is a post-resurrection example of how friends approached Jesus.

A little before Jesus died, he told his disciples he was now calling them friends instead of servants (John 15:15). Yet, when Thomas encountered him after the resurrection and finally accepted and recognized that Jesus Christ had risen, what did he say? He said: "My Lord and my God" (John 20:28)!

The truth is, as Christians, we're always accommodating as we seek to make God more relatable for those who are not in a relationship with God. This is good. After all, Jesus came, in the

---

[3] *Just Praying: Living in the Kingdom of God*. Claire Annelise Smith, 2014, DVD.

flesh, very relatable. In Jesus Christ, the harmonious relationship is restored between us and God.

Thus, God is someone to whom we can relate as with another person. However, we do so with awe, as Thomas did. God can be our friend, but revered friend. If we don't observe this, we will miss God. We will miss the vastness, the wonder, the splendor that is God and is God's. We will miss the breadth and depth of the love that God has for us; the love that sent Jesus to bridge the gap. We will reduce that love to our kind of fickle love. We will reduce that wonder to the fireworks kind of wonder. We will miss God and miss the opportunity to experience God more fully through honest, surrendered, heart praying that allows us to live with greater clarity and peace.

You see, the buddy God is too small for honest, surrendered, heart praying. The buddy God does not have the power to give us clarity and peace, regardless of how much we pray. And so we give God thanks for Jesus Christ who has shown us the way.

Leaving Jesus Behind

Isn't it sad that as Christians, followers of Jesus Christ, we know so little about him? Ah, yes, the Christmas story. Even that we don't quite get because we focus on the pageantry. Okay. What about the Easter story. Well, there are the bunny rabbits. Sometimes they get in the way. What about the life of Jesus Christ? "Ah. Right. Well, Jesus said some good stuff but you know what? I can't believe he meant half of what he said." That's what Ryder said.

Ryder considered himself a lifelong Christian. He rarely missed church. He used many of the principles in the Bible in his

Missing God

business with good results. However, when you got down to the Sermon on the Mount in Matthew 5–7, Ryder was so past that. He figured that Jesus didn't really mean all of that. It just made for good sound bites. Ryder pretty much picked the parts of Jesus' teaching that were compatible with his goals and dismissed the rest.

When we do that, like Ryder, we stumble and we falter and miss God. For Jesus Christ was God in the flesh, Immanuel, God with us, showing us how to live to please God. Jesus was the real deal.

In addition, when we leave Jesus behind for our dreams of material wealth and power, we miss God and God's reign. It's that simple. It's that pitiful.

Now this is not to say one way or another whether or not we should acquire wealth. If we're doing what God says and riches follow, let's just remember what the Psalmist said and do not set our hearts on them (Ps. 62:10). However, if we're pursuing wealth in place of the kingdom or reign of God, then we have a problem.

This pursuit of material possessions is a recipe for stress and distress. What is even worse is if we're confusing the kingdom and reign of God, which Jesus proclaimed and to which God called people, with material gain. This means that we must not have heard when Jesus said, "my kingdom is not from this world" (John18:36).

It's so easy to leave Jesus behind because Jesus gets in the way of our narrow self-centered agendas. Jesus tumbles things upside down. Jesus introduces a new way of living based on love, in which love trumps everything else. Jesus just makes us plain uncomfortable, that is, if we have a different agenda from doing what God wants. Leaving Jesus behind is equivalent to being disrespectful and irreverent. We do not revere Jesus Christ enough to follow and obey him.

So where is Jesus Christ in your life? Center or left behind? Are you missing God by leaving Jesus behind? Maybe you need a space to connect.

A Space to Connect

The world offers us surface values. Political, economic, international, and other news stories that have far reaching implications for quality of life and survival compete for space and attention with coverage of the multiple breakups and fashion wardrobes of celebrities. Furthermore, there are some people who have assigned themselves the right to decide what is a good outfit, what is beautiful, and what is not.

If we pay careful attention, we will find a close relationship between money and "beauty" in many people's eyes. This is promoted to us as the formula for happiness. People try to can and sell it to us, even in the face of evidence to the contrary.

What will happen if we watch this never-ending parade of smiling faces clad in the most expensive garb along with their never ending sagas of break ups and make ups sprinkled with empty advice? We'll find ourselves stressed and frazzled. We'll be in danger of missing ourselves. However, even more importantly than that, we will shut out some of the precious time we have in which to find a space to connect with God. This is the space that helps to keep us from missing God. This is the space that helps us to move to a deeper appreciation and reverence of God.

Missing God

The space to connect with and stop missing God is limited. As a matter of fact it seems to be shrinking as we get busier and busier. Unfortunately, this is happening at a time when we need this space more than ever, it seems.

This is part of the motivation behind this book and behind *SurrenderInPrayer*. You see, there was a time when I would say that my passion is to open the space for people to know God more. Now, I've come to realize that this is my call—to provide you with the resources and programs that will support you in making the space for that vital connection.

Connecting with the God who is real and not vague, on God's own terms, not co-opting God, whom you seek to know and revere requires space. This is a space where you'll experience God more fully, pray differently, and live with greater clarity and peace. Don't you want that?

Chapter Three

Missing Prayers

One day, Jim shared with me the burden and guilt he felt at not being where he wanted to be, where he knew he should be in his prayer life. I shared with him Romans 8:1: "There is therefore now no condemnation for those who are in Christ Jesus."

Prayer is such a wonderful gift from God. We can go to God freely at any time with confidence and candor. Yet, it remains an area in which we repeatedly stumble. This should be an area in which we press on and overcome in God's strength and grace and not a point of condemnation. If you're struggling, accept God's grace and depend on God to get you to where you need to be.

To be honest, I've experienced what Jim was going through. I thank God for where I am on this journey and the progress I've made; but it is a journey. An important lesson I've learned is that when we accept God's grace and learn to come to God with honesty, bringing all that we are and have to God, we experience God more deeply and live with greater clarity and peace. That's how I got my breakthrough. This is why you're reading this book.

Honest Prayers

We may have been taught to use certain words when praying to God. On the other hand, it is possible that while we weren't specifically taught to use such words, we've picked them up from the people around us. Somehow we feel that they will make our prayers more acceptable.

Then there's the whole issue of using prayer books. Whose words? Can you be sincere when using another person's words? What about eloquence and how others perceive our praying when we're praying in front of them? This was Colton's issue.

Colton was saying the opening prayer for the gathering. He was at his best. He chose his words carefully and they were beautiful. When he was finished, he felt that he had given a great performance. Colton loved words and praying aloud in front of others gave him another platform on which to practice and display his grasp of the language. That's where his focus lay.

Words are an important part of praying. However, could prayers be honest when we say them mindlessly and/or as a performance?

The Problem With Well-Known Phrases

Eli had a stock of words that he used in his prayers. They were good words. The thing is, he had gotten so accustomed to using these words that he said them without thinking. He wasn't really praying them. Likewise, when he heard them, they didn't really register, though he gave mental and verbal assent to them out of habit.

That's the problem, isn't it. We get so accustomed to certain words and phrases that they lose their value over time. Worse yet, we stop hearing ourselves and others say them. When this happens we find ourselves repeating words instead of really talking with God. Even though Jesus clearly said that God was looking for people who would worship God in spirit and in truth (John 4:23), our praying can become mindless. What we offer to God, therefore, is neither honest nor sincere.

An automatic, unthinking and unfeeling reaction to prayer happens more easily with well-known phrases.[4] They require less of us. They require less thought and less soul-searching. As a result, they can become a shield that stands between God and the real us.

It's hard to be sincere when we're hiding behind words. Sometimes we do this deliberately. Conversely, many times when we hide behind words we do so at a subconscious level. Either way, we're not talking to God about what's happening with us—our behaviors, thoughts, feelings, desires, interactions with others, and situations. This generally happens for five reasons—(1) shame and guilt, (2) a sense that we have to be perfect before God, (3) avoidance, (4) fear of what others would think, and (5) time.

There are times when we are so overcome with guilt about our actions that it becomes a veil when we go to pray. Instead of looking to God we focus on our guilt. We refuse to let it go and receive God's forgiveness. Sometimes we proudly wear this guilt as a badge. At other times, we're convinced that God would

---

[4]Note that we can say any word or phrase without really thinking about it when we are not focused on God.

Missing Prayers

never forgive us. Still there are times when we are overcome with shame. We are so humiliated and mortified that we would not lift our hearts to God. When this happens, we need to push past these emotions and hear Jesus say: "Neither do I condemn you. Go your way, and from now on do not sin again (John 8:11)." Then the veil will be removed and we can go to God in honesty.

Related to shame and guilt is the sense that we have to be perfect before God. You see, this keeps us on the treadmill of trying to "clean ourselves" up before we come to God. An impossible task. None of us is perfect. That's why when Jesus told those without sin to cast the first stone they all left (John 8:9). Let's just be honest with ourselves and God. We're going to mess up. We don't set out to do so, but it happens for one reason or another. When it happens, just go and tell God with all honesty. Ask God to forgive you, receive this forgiveness, and move on.

Taking our "mess ups" to God in honesty delivers us from avoidance. You see, sometimes our sense of imperfection and/or guilt and/or shame is so overwhelming that we dodge. We escape behind cliches and those well-known words and phrases. At other times, we avoid facing ourselves, because we are not happy with what we see. Sometimes we just don't want to admit who we really are and what we've really done. We have to get past and over avoidance and just tell God where we are—what we're thinking and what we're feeling.

Related to avoidance is fear. We can avoid being honest with God out of fear of others and God. However, we always have to remember that "perfect loves casts out fear" (1 John 4:18). Thus, it's important to get rid of the fear of what others will think.

How to Pray

They don't matter in this sense: When we pray we're talking with God and God accepts the spoken and unspoken words that we offer. While we're at it, let's get rid of the fear of God that makes us hesitant to be frank with God. Let's receive God's unconditional love. When we receive it, we will move past being automatic, unthinking, and unfeeling in our prayers. Instead, we will take our authentic expressions to God. We will not allow anything, even time, to get in the way of our being honest with God.

When we are rushed, it's easy to revert to well known phrases and platitudes. Avoid this trap. Of course it's better to have your intentional, focused period of praying when you do have time. Nevertheless, even when time is limited, go to God in honesty.

We can and should be honest before God. God is a loving, faithful, and compassionate parent who desires the best for us. The language we use, the meaning we put to it, and the focus with which we use it are integral to us being honest with God. The more direct we are, the more fully we will experience God. Our authenticity opens the door for surrendered, heart praying and keeps us from missing prayers.

The Problem With Prayer Books

"Is there a problem with prayer books?" some might well ask. Some of us reading this grew up with prayer books. We still use them during the worship service. For others of us, it's a strange phenomenon we don't quite understand. We grew up with extemporaneous praying. We may even have been taught

Missing Prayers

that it was wrong to use prayer books; that using them wasn't really praying from the heart.

I must confess that I was initially skeptical of the value of prayer books, having grown up in a free praying tradition. However, after being exposed to using prayer books in worship in different traditions, I found the beauty and meaning in these prayers.

As noted previously, any type of praying can become rote and automatic. Any prayer can lack sincerity. Putting God at the center of our praying is what makes the difference.

So what is the problem with prayer books? In some ways it is similar to the problem of well known phrases. The prayers in the books become prayers that we say and/or hear so often that after a while they roll over us like water on a duck's back. They do not register. It's the problem of familiarity and habit.

Am I bashing prayer books? No. I've actually written a prayer book, had prayers published in various prayer anthologies, and will doubtless write other prayer books. My main prayer book to date is *Heart Cries: 100 Prayers of Faith, Hope, and Love*. People have found meaning in these prayers.[5]

Identifying the problem with prayer books, therefore, is not to bash them but to point out the trap of us becoming so familiar with the words that we stop praying them. We thus miss honest interaction with God.

The other problem with prayer books is that they can become an escape. We can use them to get off praying with our own words, coming to God with honest prayers. Using someone

---

[5]Claire Annelise Smith, *Heart Cries: 100 Prayers of Faith, Hope, and Love,* 2014, Electronic edition.

else's prayers can be far easier and require less of us mentally and emotionally. They save us the process of getting in touch with and being honest with God about where we are, what we're doing and not doing as well as how we're treating others.

The truth is, if we're going to pray honestly we'll have to be real with ourselves, starting with our circumstances and what is happening within. For some of us this is too painful and so we hide. We hide when praying in private and we hide when praying in public. When this happens, prayer books become our escape route from doing the work of prayer.

Now, you may be like Jane. She could still feel the pain when her mother believed her abuser over her. She felt paralyzed. She had no words. Her mind was numb when she tried to talk with God. She relied on the prayers of others. However, as time went by and she got help, she started living again. Gradually, she was able to talk with God and use her own words to bring her pain and concerns to God.

Yes. There are times when you are so bereft of words that you need the prayers of prayer books. However, see this complete dependence as a temporary rather than long term option. Look forward to the time when you can offer your own honest prayers to God. Then, prayer books will be a supplement to your prayers, enlarging and enriching the language you use to come to God. When that happens, pray them from your heart.

Prayer books are a wonderful addition. However, we always have to guard against allowing them to take the place of our own honest heart cries. This is particularly true when we are praying in front of other people.

The Problem With the Audience

The problem with the audience is both real and imagined. We've been taught to put our best foot forward when in public. Hence, we figure our public praying should exhibit the best use of language. Like Colton whom we met earlier, we aspire to elocution style eloquence.

Am I faulting that style? Not if it's our honest expression before God.

What compounds this problem of the audience is that those who are often held up as exemplars of people who can pray and/or who are frequently called upon, seem to do so in lofty terms. Unconsciously we internalize that this is the way we should pray in public. This can become a barrier where we feel that we can't pray well enough to offer prayers in public.

Let me tell you about Cora. She was a farmer who had not finished high school. However, Cora prayed one of the most fervent and sincere prayers I have ever heard. She truly blessed me. Cora spoke to God and not to the other people in the prayer meeting that I was leading. She was not intimidated by my educational status because she was talking with God. What was Cora's secret? She had gone to the prayer meeting to meet with God. To do so took some effort. She had not made that journey to meet me and whomever else would be there.

What keeps us from freely offering prayers in public as Cora did? Sometimes it's as simple as not praying in private and therefore not having developed a comfort level with God that would allow us to be free to pray in public. Many times, however, it's a concern with how our prayers will be received by others. We're not sure that we pray well enough When we put

How to Pray

the spotlight on us it is easy to forget that it is to God we pray, even though it is for the edification of all who listen. Our honesty with God goes out the window. I've been there.

Releasing *Heart Cries: 100 Prayers of Faith, Hope, and Love* was a challenge for me as the author. Those are very honest prayers. Originally, they were written as private prayers and I'm a very private person. However, I shared them for two reasons. The first is that others would pray them and be blessed. In addition, I wanted to demonstrate that we can use any words, be honest, and surrender in prayer.

It's important when we go to pray, we go with the awareness that we are praying to God. This frees us as we learn more about and connect more fully with God.

Now, there is another problem with public praying. What is it? There are some people who approach prayer with a critical, judgmental attitude. This observation is based on their comments about prayers and reactions to those who have prayed aloud. These make it evident that such people do not focus on God during prayer time. They are not coming to God with honest hearts to pray alongside the person who is praying aloud.

Note that this different from when we're listening but are jarred by something someone says. If when this happens our hearts are filled with love and we are praying with honesty, here is what we would do. We will approach whomever was praying with love at an appropriate time and place. We will neither seek to shame nor condemn them.

We must avoid being hypercritical when we are praying with those who are praying aloud. At the same time, we must not allow the hypocritical person to keep us from going to God with full honesty when we are called upon to pray in public. At the end of the day, we are responsible for our hearts and not theirs. Let's not allow "the audience" to keep us from missing prayer.

Surrendered Prayers

For some of us, the word "surrender" is more easily said than practiced. For others of us, we baulk at the word. For some odd reason it suggests to us giving up all what we hold dear, including that precious and often misunderstood concept of freedom.

Even though we would give mental and verbal assent to the understanding that God knows everything, knows more about us than we could know and clearly sees what is ahead, we still stumble when it comes to surrendering to God. We don't talk about it. We avoid the word. The other word we avoid is "submit." We won't embrace the concept.

Those of us who are willing to talk about surrendering to God often show by our actions and how we deal with situations that we're not doing so. We don't check with God. We just go ahead and do our thing using the ways in which our culture says we should react to and deal with situations. Our prayer language also indicates where we are in regards to surrendering to God. Many times, it will show that we are not yielded. Like the Pharisee in Jesus' parable in Luke 18:10–14, we go to God full of ourselves. We are so full of how good we are and what we want that we will not give in to God. Why would we, when we're already super worthy and more?

Our lack of or limited surrender is often based on misconceptions of what and who this Christian life is about. Our prayers reflect this. Let's address these misconceptions since they are keeping us from experiencing God more fully and living with greater clarity and peace.

Prayer is Not About . . . Us

Natalie prayed often. She strongly believed in the power of prayer. She was not afraid to ask God for what she wanted. And did she ever want. Truth be told, Natalie didn't ask for much. However, she was very clear on what she wanted God to do. All she wanted from God was a safe, comfortable, and predictable life. Oh. She also wanted God to protect those who were close to her.

It's wonderful that we can take all our cares and petitions to God. Prayer is such a privilege and gift. The Bible tells us to cast all our cares on God (1 Pet. 5:7). Honest, surrendered praying dictates that we do just that. However, there is a deep misconception that is often inherent in our prayer. What is it? It is simply this: We are the center, not God. We see this example of me-centered actions and prayer in Jonah.[6]

Prayer should be about God. Why? Because our lives are now hid in Christ and centered on God (Col. 3:2–3). Thus, every aspect of our life, including our praying should be on how we can please God. This is the basis of surrendered prayer.

This does not mean that we do not ask God for basic aspects of life. However, we should be attending and attentive to what God wants for us and those around us so that what we ask is in

---

[6]Smith, *Prayer Guide: Finding Your True North* (Mission KS: SurrenderInPrayer, 2014), 8–9.

accordance with what God wants. We seek to please God in our entire lives, including our praying. We recognize God's supremacy and God's authority. That's surrendered praying at a basic level.

In addition, God has a wide circle. We read that God loves the world. That's huge. Nowhere do we read that the world loves God, or God loves the world because the world loves God. On the contrary, we read that we love because God first loved us (1 John 4:19). What does this mean for our praying?

Pray for people you know and people you don't know. Widen your circle of care. Pray for people you like and don't like and those who don't like you. Reflect God who is love. Identify various community and global situations and specific parts of the world for which you will pray, as God leads. Surrender your prayers to be in line with God's circle.

Decentering self in these ways will keep our prayers from lacking what is vital. There are others ways in which our prayers are missing.

Prayer is Not About ... What

There is some identity confusion between God and Santa Claus. You see, as children we were taught to make a list for Santa. Depending on our circumstances, we may have grown up with Santa granting our every wish. Even when we were not that "fortunate" we still internalized the script that Santa is the giver of gifts—that was Santa's job. Here's another example.

You may have taken your child or have been taken as a child to the Santa in a store. The child goes to this Santa for two things. To get a picture with Santa and to receive a gift. That's it. Once again, the relationship with Santa is one way.

Unfortunately, this can be our approach to prayer, where the relationship with God is about the "what." What can I get God to give me? It's one way. Even when we give to God, it is with the expectation of getting. That's still one-way. There's no genuine relationship and interaction. God has indeed become Santa to us. God is a what and not someone to whom we surrender and come before with honest, surrendered, heart prayers.

It is very sad that we would go to God on the basis of what God will give us. God offers so much more—a relationship.

When we go to God to get, the unique work of Jesus Christ in dying and rising for our sins is lost. For some of us it's like this: "Sin? Why are you talking about sin? No. We don't bother about that anymore. Come to God and reign with Christ and you'll get all this stuff. Just ask. Ask with enough faith and you'll get it." Lord, forgive us and help us. We have made light of the supreme sacrifice of your Son Jesus Christ. We have turned your free grace and ensuing relationship into a "what."

Many will turn away from God when they realize that it's all a big con. God is in the giving business but God is not in the Santa business. God invites us into relationship, gives us grace, and delivers us from the power of sin and death (Romans 5:20–21, 1 Corinthians 15:54–56). If we think prayer is about the "what," we're definitely missing prayer. We're definitely not surrendered to God and therefore our prayers will be self-centered, as those of a spoilt child.

Prayer and Your Starting Point

It all comes down to our starting point. Are we starting with us or with God?

Caleb prayed and prayed. One day, he stopped and thought about his prayers. He realized that he never really thought about God when he was praying. Even though ostensibly he was praying to God, he was focused on what he was saying, which was fine. However, he wasn't praying as if God was a vital being. God wasn't even in his mind.

Surrendered praying requires that when we come to God we start with God at the center. We bring all that we are to God and we come on God's terms. Why?

God is. God is the great "I am who I am" (Exod. 3:14). God is the One who exists through all eternity, who created the universe (Gen. 1), who is faithful even when we are not faithful (2 Tim. 2:13), who loves eternally (Jer. 31:3), and who loves us to the point of death (Ephesians 5:1–2). Yes, this God came in Jesus Christ to die and rise for our sins and our salvation. This God deserves no lesser place than the beginning and center of our universe.

Starting our prayers with us and what we want is to miss prayer because we're starting by missing God. One may even say we're starting by "dissing" God.

Consider Jesus Christ. Jesus began with God.

How do we do this? How do we begin with God? Consider Kole.

Each day, Kole started the day with the same fervent prayer: "I thank you God that I am the head and not the tail, that you have made me more than a conqueror. I ask you to take all negative people out of my life. Give me victory in every situation. Let your face shine on me and prosper all my endeavors. Thank you for a favorable outcome in everything I do. In the mighty name of Jesus. Amen."

Do you pray like Kole? I suspect that there is a bit of Kole in all of us. On the surface, Kole's prayer is a great one. However, here's the deal. Kole's prayer starts with Kole. It does not recognize God, other than throwing God's name in there. Neither does it reflect the great commandments to love God and love neighbor as we love ourselves. This is because not only does it start with Kole, but it also ends with Kole. God is there for Kole's convenience. There is no surrender.

In our praying we need to start with God and end with God. In the middle, our prayers should reflect the great commandments as we surrender to God. Let's not be missing prayers.

Heart Prayers

The Bible is filled with people who offered up heart prayers to God. There are three memorable in *Heart Prayers: When You Know That God is All You Have*.[7] They are Hannah, Moses, and Jesus. Yes. These three were not only honest and surrendered in the midst of their own desires, but their prayers came from deep within, involving all of who they were.

Take Jesus in the Garden. Yes. He was going to the cross. However, he had this moment when the enormity of it hit him.

---

[7] Smith, *Heart Cries*, DVD.

Missing Prayers

He went to God in complete honesty. "Grieved and agitated," he poured out his hear to God and ultimately surrendered saying, "if this cannot pass unless I drink it, your will be done"(Matt. 26:36–42). What an example for us!

In the *SurrenderInPrayer* ministry, "heart" is the deepest place from which our will and emotions spring which influence our thinking, speaking, and acting. At the same time, the heart is prone to sin and error and needs to be constantly renewed by God. The new creation we receive in Jesus Christ includes the heart. This understanding of heart is influenced by the way the Bible uses the word.

Knowing Your Limits

Layla loved music. She knew all the tunes that they sang in church. Layla would often be found sitting in the front singing lustily, encouraging whomever was leading the singing during worship. She wanted to lead the music during worship so badly but no one ever asked her. Fortunately, Layla was not upset. You see, Layla knew herself. She knew that she could not carry a tune.

Knowing yourself includes knowing your limitations. Yes. You can overcome limitations but first you have to know them.

It's difficult now. We're in an age when everyone knows everything, can do everything, and is always right. At least that's the impression we get from the media and as we hear stories of what's happening in our schools and other institutions. When everyone is right and everyone knows everything, here are some things that follow.

How to Pray

We find it hard to accept that other people know more than we do in some areas. Relatedly, accepting another's authority becomes an issue. In addition, we begin to lack the basic courtesies such as apologizing. If we're always right, we're never going to need to apologize. Moreover, we'll become frustrated those times when everyone cannot participate and based on the criteria used, we are not selected. The result of all this is stress and insecurity. Consequently, knowing and understanding ourselves, accepting our strengths and limitations makes for more harmonious living both internally and with others.

It's not only in our day-to-day dealings that we find it difficult to accept our limitations. The myth that we know everything and can do everything seeps over into our dealings with God. The result is that we find it difficult to surrender to God. This myth also explains why we hold back our heart prayers. Having limitations mean we're vulnerable. If we will not admit to having limitations we will not allow ourselves to be vulnerable before anyone. However, like it or not, God is bigger than we are being omnipotent. God knows more than we do, being omniscient.

Then there's the issue of our motivations. So often, we start off with the right motives but somewhere along the line they become skewed and what we're doing becomes about us and how we will benefit. We seek to love purely yet fall short of the consistent standard Jesus set for love. We quickly become turned inward.

In addition, our will is in a battle with God for control of our lives. If you don't think this is so, just have a sense of God asking you to do something that requires you giving up what is important to you. Step back, and witness your ensuing internal and external struggle to do it. Of course you may not believe that God would ask you to do that. Or, if you do, there will be many around you to tell you otherwise.

We are limited in many ways. Without knowing, acknowledging, and accepting our limitations we will be missing in our praying. Consequently, we will not go to God with our whole hearts. We will always keep a piece locked away for ourselves because God will not be big enough to deserve it all. We will not seek the cleansing and forgiveness that we need from God. Thus, we will miss that God is adequate for all our needs and situations.

The irony is that God is the One who can best help us to address, move around, and move past our limitations. We will be missing in our praying when we ignore our limitations.

Knowing Your Attitude

There are some attitudes that reinforce the barrier to heart praying that has been imposed by our inability to accept our limitations. These attitudes are fast gaining currency in today's life. Conversely, there are attitudes that help us to be more open to our need of God and to utter heart prayers. We can learn from Amelia.

Amelia had won several awards and accolades. However, unless someone told you about them, you would not know. Amelia never mentioned them. In her interactions with others she was genuine, loving, and humble regardless of the other person's station in life. At the same time, she was confident. She knew who she was. If you asked her, she would tell you that it all came from knowing who she was in God.

When Amelia prayed, these attitudes shone through. She approached God with sincerity and humility. You heard her love and reverence for God as she approached God with the confidence of a child with a parent of whose love and care she was assured. Moreover, Amelia was fully present and her prayers were thoughtful and attentive to the working of the Spirit of God.

We're a whole person. Unless there is some interruption in our psychological structure how we are in one arena of life carries over to the other arenas. Our attitudes with people often reflect our attitude with God. That's why we need to check and know our attitudes and see if they may be hindering our ability not only to offer prayers from our heart but also to offer honest and surrendered prayers.

We need to note that heart prayers may or may not be honest and surrendered. However, honest prayers that are surrendered will always come from the heart. Nevertheless, without the right attitude, we will be missing prayers.

These attitudes are simple and basic. But, as I mentioned at the beginning of the chapter, they are fast losing currency. Here they are: genuineness, humility, love, mindfulness, and confidence in God.

What this means is that we are honest and sincere in our dealings with each other and God. If we're living as God desires, we will have nothing to hide. Next, humility comes from understanding who we are before God and realizing that as David said, all that we have comes from God (1 Chr. 29:14). The

Missing Prayers

new life comes from God, thus if we're going to boast let it be in the cross of Jesus Christ (Gal. 6:14).

At the same time, we move with confidence because we are grounded in the love of God. Therefore, whatever space we inhabit, we are fully present, attuned to God working and speaking to us through the Spirit.

When we know our attitudes, we will avoid missing prayers and we will also be more fully whom God created us to be.

The Space to Be You

It's unfortunate that as important as honest, surrendered heart praying is, there aren't always the collective spaces in which to do it. In other words, there aren't enough collective spaces in which to be fully you before God.

If only . . . Daisy went to church every Sunday. She enjoyed the worship and meeting others. She felt that she was learning a lot. She was also making connections. Daisy attended Sunday School. It was fun and a better place for connecting. The Sunday School Class was a tight bunch and everyone looked out for each other. However, something was still missing. If only . . .

What Daisy was looking for and wasn't finding was a place where people of faith shared deeply about their faith journey. It was okay to be concerned and support each other in matters of health and the practicalities of daily living. However, Daisy felt that she could get that at other places like the Kiwanis and other clubs. Where could she find a confidential space to examine her faith journey, to be encouraged, and encourage others as she sought to live more as God wanted, as Jesus showed? Where

53

How to Pray

could she go to find people who wanted to pray more and experience God more and live surrendered lives?

I know what it is like to be without people with whom to pray. The truth is, many people in our churches withdraw from praying. It is my prayer God would use this book and the work we do at *SurrenderInPrayer*; that our programs and books would allay these fears and give people the confidence and tools to pray. At the same time, I'm realistic enough to know that some people just aren't interested in praying. That's sad. They have no idea what they're missing and they continue to muddle through life, totally stressed, never knowing what to do when life hits, as it does.

However, for those who want to pray more and/or learn to pray *SurrenderInPrayer* is here. You will find that some of our programs include a time for prayer. You'll also find on our website the opportunity to schedule a free slot for prayer and conversation around prayer. Honest, surrendered heart praying is too vital for a fuller experience of God leading to clarity and peace. We must provide this type of support.

That's why *SurrenderInPrayer* is the place where those who want to experience God more fully do so through honest, surrendered, heart praying and live with greater clarity and peace in this world. It's about God. It's about you. We don't want you to be missing prayers.

Chapter Four

Living Wholly

"When you pray, say:
Father, hallowed be your name.
  Your kingdom come.
  Give us each day our daily bread.
  And forgive us our sins,
    for we ourselves forgive everyone indebted to us.
  And do not bring us to the time of trial" (Luke 11:2-4).

Harper had recited The Lord's Prayer her entire life. She had learned it as a child. But that's just it. She had said it but rarely prayed it; rarely thought about its context and meaning. As a result, it was easy for her to say it mindlessly.[8]

The kernel of the Lord's Prayer was written in response to the disciples' request. They wanted Jesus to teach them how to pray (Luke 11:1). But why? Surely they had been praying their entire lives. They were Jews, after all; religious people. What was it that they saw and heard in Jesus that would make them ask him to teach them to pray? It was a request that implied that either Jesus was praying in a way that was different from what they had always known and/or that something was different after

---

[8]In *Just Praying: Living the Kingdom of God*, we give you the tools to take another look at the Lord's prayer so that you pray it mindfully, with insight into what it meant then and what it means now. *Just Praying: Living the Kingdom of God*, Smith, 2014, DVD.

How to Pray

he had prayed. We say this because they asked Jesus to teach them to pray when he had just finished praying.

The answer to the question as to why the disciples made this request can only come from Jesus' life and the prayer itself. Here are four things that are clearly identifiable from even a cursory look at Jesus' life and The Lord's Prayer:

1. Jesus prayed often by himself. Luke tells us that "he would withdraw to deserted places and pray" (Luke 5:16). Could it be that there was something different about him that the disciples attributed to his praying?
2. Jesus' prayer show intimacy. The prayers for which we have words demonstrate an intimate connection with God, such as he teaches in the Lord's Prayer.[9] It's hard to fake intimacy.
3. Jesus' prayers show honesty, surrender, and are offered from his heart. He says what he's feeling and thinking, but ultimately leaves the answer to God.
4. Jesus' prayers, including the Lord's Prayer, acknowledge and focus on God, showing concern for others. They are never about him but about God and God's glory.

Therefore, to learn how to pray we must follow Jesus and like the disciples, learn from him. But before we continue, let's

---

[9] Here are some places where we find Jesus praying to God with intimacy: Matt. 11:25–27, Luke 10:21–22, Luke 23:34, John 11:41-42, John 12:27-28, John 17.

Living Wholly

look at where we are in this book, *How to Pray: Living Wholly Through Honest, Surrendered, Heart Praying*.

We have identified the missing parts. We've seen how hidden fears, lack of self-knowledge, and the quest for security on our own terms keep us from experiencing God more fully. Furthermore, we've explored how we miss God when we fail to go to God on God's own terms with due reverence and instead cultivate our own God that lacks specificity and depth. Thus, we miss God when we seek to make God into our image and leave Jesus behind.

In addition, we've looked at how our prayers miss honesty when words become familiar and/or we are anxious about being acceptable to our audience. We've also seen how we miss God and our prayers when we're about us and not about God and giving to God what is due to God. Moreover, we turn our backs on the freedom God gives as we refuse to acknowledge and accept our limitations and cultivate the right attitudes to God.

Now you have a choice. You can decide that this is not for you and close the book at this point. However, you can decide that yes, you want to know how to pray with honest, surrendered, heart prayers. You want to know this so that you can experience God more fully and live wholly with clarity and peace in this world.

Let's continue this journey of discipleship together in following Jesus Christ's way of praying and living.

How to Pray

Finding the Wilderness and the Mountain

Isabella decided to go on a wilderness retreat. Truth to tell, she wasn't going into rugged terrain. For her, the wilderness represented a place away from the regular hustle and bustle of life. It would be a place away from her myriad responsibilities. Sometimes she imagined that she had climbed the mountain and was now at the top. From her vantage point, she looked out over the expanse of God's creation and breathed in the mountain air. All Isabella really wanted was to simply slow down, pray, reconnect with God and find herself again. This imaginative journey helped her to do so and fulfill her longing to simply "breathe" in the midst of life's challenges.

Sometime or the other, life is going to come crashing down on you like a ton of bricks. This may happen because you are dealing with an illness or the loss of someone or something that you hold dear. It may happen because of the burden you carry for others and the situations in the world. It could also come from the stress of caring for others in your family and/or at work. Or, you're faced with a major decision. Perhaps the weight of all of your responsibilities suddenly hits you. Whatever, the cause you are overwhelmed. Can somebody raise their hand along with me? Yes. Overwhelm is real. That's why it's important, like Isabella, to find the wilderness and/or the mountain.

The wilderness and the mountain were real in Jesus' life. Those were the places where he went to pray. Evidently, he valued times alone with God. He made them happen, even in the midst of the life crisis of his impending death. To be like Jesus and do this sometimes calls for us to learn, relearn, and reboot.

Living Wholly

Learning, Relearning, and Rebooting

Henry had never been a good listener. He didn't stop talking long enough to listen, for starters. When he did stop speaking, his mind was racing so he didn't hear anyone. Needless to say, Henry had a problem with the concept and practice of listening to God. However, he knew that if he wanted to grow more in God he would have to practice listening.

Henry started with baby steps, being still to listen for a minute, then two, then five, then ten, then . . . . He also found that it helped to start with the Scriptures and prayer before going into silent-listening mode.

For many of us, listening is a challenge; that is listening that hears at a deep level. We've become accustomed to listening on the surface, throwing out a quick answer that does not go to the root of what has been said. This approach to listening, let's just call it what it is—superficial—is all around us, including in the public sphere. It impacts how we go to God.

Superficial listening requires nothing of us. We don't need to embrace the other person in such a way that we touch their heart and they touch ours. We don't need to dignify them by seeking to understand where they are coming from. We just go for the quick exchange that benefits us, even if they never benefit. In the same way, we go to God for the quick exchange to get our fix. What about God?

You may say, "What do you mean by, 'what about God?' I'm talking about me and my needs. Of course God, is in there somewhere." Is that all you want from God? Don't you want to hear what God would say to you?

Listening to God requires going beyond superficial listening. Hence the challenge. God is not on our time frame, waiting to throw a quick answer to our quick question. We have to learn to hear God, and/or relearn as the case may be.

Now, there are times when God does send the quick response. However, deep hearing comes from intentionally dwelling with God and learning to hear God again. Then, we're more attuned to those times when God will send the quick response.

When it comes to listening to God, which is it for you? Is it learning to hear God for the first time or relearning to hear God? Or, you're already practicing deep hearing, which is wonderful. For many of us, however, if we want to hear God even when God does not prop up our egos we have to start with the desire to do so. We then follow this desire to hear with a reboot.

There are times when the software on my computer goes crazy on me for no apparent reason. Sometimes I can figure it out and sort it out in the moment. At other times, I have to close all my programs, shut down the computer and reboot. 99.9 percent of the time that works.

Rebooting gives the system a chance to reset itself. When we've gotten out of the practice of dwelling with and listening to God, we are in need of a reset. Let's just stop for a moment and shut out everything and get to the basics of our life with God. That's why I offer retreats through *SurrenderInPrayer*. One of the things this reset does is to allow us to tune in.

Tuning Out: Quiet Places Without

For some of us, finding a quiet place is easy. All we have to do is to make the time. Silence comes naturally for us. In addition, we live by ourselves and so control when sounds come on and off. Moreover, we are surrounded by people who also value silence. Thus, we do not have to deal with a 24-hour stream of noise. Is that you?

Or, are you someone who is uncomfortable with silence? For some silence is threatening as our thoughts take over and these are not always happy thoughts. For others, we've just always been in an environment of constant sound. Hence, silence is unfamiliar and unnerving. We may even find that noises help us to focus. It is possible, however, that we are like Alyssa.

Alyssa longed for silence. However, no one else in the household seemed to value it. The constant occurrence of people speaking and the background noise of the television that played practically 24-7 were irritants for her. She often felt that she could not hear herself think. Sometimes she wanted to scream because of the noise around her that never allowed her to feel settled within. She felt as if she couldn't pray with any depth. She couldn't focus.

Alyssa realized that she had to act. She had already tried complaining to no avail. Hence, she saw herself having two viable options available. Alyssa could either get up very early before everyone else and take advantage of the narrow window of time when all was quiet. Or, she could leave home regularly and go to a park or church or . . . any place that allowed the "sound of silence." Somehow she had to find her mountain.

How to Pray

Are you Alyssa? Perhaps you're not Alyssa but you have friends who are Alyssa. Your environment does not lend itself to the quiet places in which you can tune in to God more deeply. It is possible, of course, that you are closer to Maya.

Maya had small children. They kept her busy. Sometimes she didn't know if she was coming or going. And she was tired. Before she went back to work after the last baby, she had her focused time with God when her children and husband had left and the baby was asleep. Now that she was back at work, it wasn't that easy. Some days, she had to find this time in increments. Get up a little earlier, carve out some time during lunch . . . .

"So what's the big deal about finding this focused prayer time in which I tune out just about everything? Can't I pray without this time?" Of course. However, consider this.

Let's start with Jesus who made a practice of going aside to pray with God. Look at his life of love and service as well as the wisdom with which he dealt with his opposers, accusers, and just life! His life makes a strong case for going to the wilderness and the mountain.

The quiet or silent places allow us to encounter God in a deeper way. Think about the difference in how well you know someone with whom you spend time versus someone to whom you say hello everyday and keep going, or at the most have a very brief conversation.

You know much more about the person with whom you spend time. Sometimes you do the talking. However, to know them you do a lot of listening. You ask questions. Sometimes you just spend time soaking in their presence, comfortable in a shared bond.

Living Wholly

It can be like that with God. Turning to the quiet places without allows you to better create the space to cultivate a deep relationship with God. You know God more. You hear what God wants of you better. You are wiser and stronger to deal with all that comes at you in life, and you are empowered to love and serve. Find the time. Find the wilderness and the mountain. It matters.

There's one other point that's very important. These quiet places honor God. You're saying to God that God is important enough to you for you to step away from the noise and bustle to be with God. As a result, you will turn off all distractions, including the cell phones and other gadgets to be with God. It's about love and honor.

Now, it's important to note that God is not hovering over you with a big stick saying, "Find your wilderness/mountain; make time for me or else . . . !" Grace still abounds. However, if you value God, your relationship with God, and desire to know and do as God wants, you will find the quiet places without. Be as creative as you need to be to find these places. They will ultimately lead you to finding quiet within.

Tuning in: Quiet Places Within

It's in the quiet places that we learn to still ourselves within. That's where we find that center that anchors us and gives us clarity and peace. Then, we take it with us so that even in the clamor of life we can tap into it, find ourselves again and know in which direction to go.

Declan woke up early while it was still quiet. This was his time with God. The only sound he could hear was the singing of the birds. As he heard them, he remembered Jesus' words: "Look at the birds of the air; they neither sow nor reap nor gather into barns, and yet your heavenly Father feeds them. Are you not of more value than they" (Matt. 6:26)? He sought to quiet himself and focus on God as the loving, providing parent, but his thoughts kept racing as he remembered all that he had to do that day as well as all the bills that were due.

Declan kept coming back to this same verse in Matthew 6:26 to quiet himself so that he could tune in within. Gradually, he began to sense God's presence with him. He began to experience the peace that could only come from God. With perseverance, he was now quieted within and ready to listen.

Tuning in is not as simple as it sounds, at least for most of us. Even when we have dealt with the outer environment, we still have to deal with the mind and our emotions that can keep us from finding the quiet place within. Let's get some help from the Psalmist who said:

> O Lord, my heart is not lifted up,
>   my eyes are not raised too high;
> I do not occupy myself with things
>   too great and too marvelous for me.
> But I have calmed and quieted my soul,
>   like a weaned child with its mother;
>   my soul is like the weaned child that is with me.
> O Israel, hope in the Lord
>   from this time on and forevermore (Psalm 131).

In laying this out, the Psalmist points to one of the things that prevents us from tuning in to God. It is a big deal, because it

Living Wholly

also impacts our ability to tune out, even though this section is concerned with tuning it. What is it? Our position before God accompanied by our level of trust in God. Let me give you an example.

Isla was very anxious. She was afraid of missing out. She always expected that something would go wrong and wanted to be the first to know. Even when it was time to pray, she kept her phone on. She had one ear attuned to hear the phone ring. She kept waiting for the phone to ring with news that would take her away from this time. Tuning in wasn't something she particularly wanted to do.

In addition, like Declan, Isla had lots of thoughts racing through her head as she thought of all that had gone wrong and could go wrong; all that she had to do. However, she gave in to these. She didn't try to quiet herself and tune in. For Isla, it was enough that she showed up to pray. After that . . . she simply would not quiet herself.

Lila also liked to know what was happening. She knew that anything could go wrong at any time. She had children. She had people depending on her. However, unlike Isla, she figured that if she gave God the time she had set aside, God would take care of everything. God was that loving parent. Like the Psalmist in Psalm 131, she chose to exercise her trust in God and tune in. This particular day, however, she was finding it hard to find the quiet place within. Nevertheless, she persevered, for she knew that it was there. She would find it again.

The first step in quieting ourselves involves how we relate to God. Jesus constantly used the parent-child image in relation to us and God. God is the good parent who gives good gifts (Matt. 7:11) and who will not forget God's children (Isa. 49:15). Yes.

How to Pray

This image is also present in the Hebrew Bible/Old Testament. The invitation is to see ourselves as children of a loving, generous parent, and in doing so trust this parent. Then extend this trust into our time with God so that we tune out the mental and emotional distractions to tune in fully.

This is the first step to tuning in. However, it does not guarantee that we will be able to tune in immediately. Some are able to so. Others of us have to combine other activities like focusing on Scripture and centering prayer,[10] to get us there.

Here is how we can do as Declan did and use Scripture. First, we identify a specific verse as our centering point. Whenever our minds wander, we say or read that verse to re-center. Or, we may have various Scripture verses and passages that we draw on. Either way, we start with and/or use Scripture to help us tune in.

Another tuning in "activity" is having a time of praise and worship unto almighty God. For some people, these two are one and the same. However, I make a distinction in this way. Praise incorporates thankfulness for what God has done. This includes God giving us grace, mercy, and love as well as specific situations in which we have experienced God's provision, healing, deliverance, and so forth.

---

[10]"Centering Prayer is a method of silent prayer that prepares us to receive the gift of contemplative prayer, prayer in which we experience God's presence within us, closer than breathing, closer than thinking, closer than consciousness itself. This method of prayer is both a relationship with God and a discipline to foster that relationship" "Centering Prayer," Centering Prayer, accessed May 28, 2015, http://www.centeringprayer.com/.

Worship, on the other hand, is based solely on God's character. Worship is an invitation to let go of self and exalt the One who is above all; the One who created everything. It's an invitation to explore and glory in God's infinitude before which we pale as finite beings. It's an opportunity to catch a glimpse of God's holiness before which we are awed that God dwells with and in us. Worship is an invitation to encounter and experience the indescribable that is larger than we are and which draws us in. It is what we so desperately crave and seek in human celebrities and shows. However, through worship we encounter and experience the other-worldly in life-giving and life-transforming ways that take us within and then send us out to know, to serve, to be like Jesus Christ. Worship is Isaiah 6:3, 5, 7–8:

> Holy, holy, holy is the Lord of hosts;
> the whole earth is full of his glory" . . .
> And I said: "Woe is me! I am lost, for I am a man of unclean lips, and I live among a people of unclean lips; yet my eyes have seen the King, the Lord of hosts!" . . .The seraph touched my mouth with it and said: "Now that this has touched your lips, your guilt has departed and your sin is blotted out." Then I heard the voice of the Lord saying, "Whom shall I send, and who will go for us?" And I said, "Here am I; send me!"

Indeed, worship helps us to tune in and quiet ourselves so that we get a larger vision of God, a more accurate understanding of ourselves, hear what God wants us to do, and are empowered to respond in the affirmative.

As we close this section on "Finding the Wilderness and the Mountain," I am aware that I haven't addressed retreats and other forms of communal tuning in and out. These are important. However, in this book, *How to Pray*, I am focused on empowering the individual person in their particular environment. They will in turn enrich the corporate gatherings.

There's a New Ruler in Town

Worship leads us to recognize that there's a new ruler in town. It's as if we say, "Move over self. I'm dethroning you."

Robin was as sharp as a tack in more ways than one. She was smart, highly motivated, and knew how to get things done. When she showed up people gave her room. When she spoke, people took notice. Robin had gotten accustomed to being the one in charge. It was hard for her to follow anyone because she was the one who knew more and was normally right. Interestingly enough, this carried over into her spiritual life. Robin found it hard to follow Jesus Christ and do what God wanted. She wasn't sure that she was ready for a new ruler. It showed in her prayers during which she focused on herself and what she wanted God to do. Robin had failed to recognize the high quality pearl that was in front of her.

What Would You Give for a Pearl?

Of course, to answer this question, you first have to recognize the pearl. In today's terms, you'd need to know the difference between the cosmetic pearl and the AAA pearl. Then you could say what you would give for it. Everyone does not

Living Wholly

have this type of knowledge and discernment. However, there was a merchant who did.

In Matthew 13: 45–46 we read about this merchant: "Again, the kingdom of heaven is like a merchant in search of fine pearls; on finding one pearl of great value, he went and sold all that he had and bought it."

First of all, the merchant realized that what was in front of him was exceptional. It was different. Not only that, he understood that it was worth more than anything he possessed. Thus, he knew that when he sold everything, he would get back more than what he sold.

It raises a question: Can you truly recognize the kingdom of God and still hold back on giving everything you have, including yourself, to God? After all, Jesus was describing the kingdom in active terms—once you've discerned it, you give everything to gain it. In other words, you give up all that you are and have to come under God's rule.

You can be like Robin above, or you can be like Emmett.

Emmett's parents were atheists. He had never attended church. He really didn't know anything about God other than snippets he'd heard from time to time. One day, however, Emmett came across a Bible. He started to read it. While he was reading the Bible Emmett was convicted by the Holy Spirit. He recognized his pearl of great value and became a Christian, just like that. He put his life under a new ruler, put aside his ambitions, and sought to serve God and do what God wanted. Subsequently, his prayers were not about what he wanted out of life but what God wanted of his life.

Do you want God to rule your life? Seriously. Do you see in God's reign the pearl of great value or do you see yourself as the pearl of great value and God as the lesser, cosmetic pearl? If it's the latter, you really have no reason to give up everything for you are already everything. But, could it be so?

I have a feeling you'll say no. You'll say that without a doubt God, the reign of God, is the pearl of great value. However, too often our behavior suggests that we have not recognized the supreme value of God's reign. Hence, we're still focused on running our lives with some input from God and every expectation that God will do what we want. This goes back to the different ways in which we miss God.

So, what does it mean to run our own lives? Here's what it looks like. We set our goals without finding out what God wants. Our standards of success are aligned with those of our socio-economic order and not with the kingdom of God. We pay lip service to servanthood but really when we serve we do things that satisfy us and/or show that we are above others. We talk a good talk about humility but get offended when we're not given "the best seats." We pray accordingly.

Here's the deal. We can continue to run our lives as we see fit, with all the stress that comes with that. Or, we can let a new ruler into the town of our lives and sell all for this pearl of great value, and decrease stress while we're at it. Thus, when we pray we put our prayers under God's rule. That's how Jesus prayed. Once we do that, we'll have a solid foundation. Why?

Praying On the Solid Rock

To be under God's rule is to first of all desire what God desires. We're seeking to know and do what God wants. That's called obedience. That is the rock.

Living Wholly

Earlier, we determined that listening and hearing are not automatic. For some of us we have to work at it. Here is the thing, though. It is one thing to listen and hear. It's quite another to act on what we hear. Yet, therein lies our ability to remain standing in all times and seasons. If we can hear and follow through in obedience, we will stand. If we cannot, we will fall when the pressures and stresses of life come (Matt. 7:24–27). Look what happened to Jace.

Chase asked Jace what was wrong. Jace shook his head to indicate that nothing was wrong. Chase knew differently, but wisely left it alone.

The truth is, Jace was struggling internally. For the first time he was confronted with the depth of his commitment to Jesus Christ.

You see, Jace had always assumed that he was fully committed. He sang, "On Christ the solid rock I stand" with glad abandon. He was morally upright. He was regular in church. He paid his tithes and offerings. Outside of church, people around Jace knew that Jace was dependable. Jace was moving up the ranks at his place of employment. He had it made and he owed it all to Jesus Christ. He thanked God frequently for blessing him.

Jace was regular, punctual, and conscientious at work. Then, one day everything changed. He would never forget that day. He went to work as usual only to learn that he had been fired. No reason was given. Jace was worried. He could no longer make ends meet. Jace felt as if God had abandoned him. Now, when he attended church, he was just going through the motions. His heart was no longer in it. What had happened to all the blessings God had promised him? The storms were on and Jace was in danger of falling.

How to Pray

What does this have to do with listening, hearing and obeying Jesus Christ? You see, it goes back to setting the socio-economic standards of our day as markers of success. When we do this, it becomes that much harder to hear what God would have us be and do. We go to God assuming that what we see as upward mobility is what God has for us and that it equates with God blessing us. We assume that God would never tell us anything or allow anything in our lives that is contrary to these yardsticks. Moreover, we assume that these are our due. Thus, we are stuck in prayers that massage our egos and validate our assumptions as we saw when we looked at ways in which our prayers are missing. What we need, instead, is faithful listening, hearing, and obeying.

Drop the assumptions. Be like Jesus. Constantly seek to know what God wants and then give everything in order to follow it. When the storms come you will not be moved because you are acting in accordance with what God has told you to do.

In addition, even if some flicker of doubt seeps in, you will still stand freely on the solid rock.

Living freely

When we've built on the solid rock, we're free to live without worry and fear. Yes. I know. Sometimes we think that worrying is our right. We have those times when we think that these words of Jesus are unrealistic: "do not worry about your life . . ." (Matt. 6:25). We forget that God does not promise us "sunshine and roses" every day of our lives. Moreover, Jesus said to count the cost of following him, for there is a cross

Living Wholly

involved (Luke 14:25-33). Thus worry free living under the new ruler is not the absence of challenges in our lives.

It comes back, therefore, to how we know, understand, and accept God and God's love and reign. If we know that God is trustworthy and we're committed to following Jesus Christ wherever and however, we'll be fine. We will not need to stress. However, if we're committed to our version of God and what our due is, we will be stressed. Not only that. We'll be fearful and miss the freedom that is ours.

Griffin looked at Gemma and shook his head. "Such a loser," he thought. He couldn't understand why Gemma had given up her job at a prestigious law firm to go and work for a non-profit advocacy group. The move was as dumb as a box of rocks.

Gemma looked through the window. She shook her head and laughed. She felt so free it was unreal. She experienced a sense of calm and serenity. She was done with climbing up the ladder to "success." She'd finally stopped struggling with God and done what God wanted. Yes. She'd had to make changes to her lifestyle, but she rested in the security of knowing she was right where God wanted her to be—working with the non-profit advocacy group. Some months were uncertain, but God always came through.

Was she now going to go on a crusade to tell everyone they should leave the high pressure corporate world? No. Each person needed to listen, hear, and obey God for themselves.

You can be like Griffin looking down on everyone who doesn't follow your concept of the good life. If this concept is outside of what God wants for you, you will be carrying the stress that goes with forever climbing up and seeking to hold on to it all. Or, you can be like Gemma, perfectly free and content knowing that you are right where you need to be. In any case, recent history continues to show that success on the world's terms is not secure. The ladder breaks or is pulled from under you. The money vanishes overnight.

Thus, it is not the material things that give the freedom. Freedom comes from God. This means that even if things go inexplicably wrong, once you know that you are doing what God wants, you maintain your focus. Just take a look at Jesus. On his way to the cross he still prayed, "not what I want but what you want" (Matt. 26:39). Then, he rose up and freely continued his journey to the cross. He had started in the right place.

Living Wholly with Clarity and Peace

I'm sure that you would agree that starting at the right place goes a long way to ensuring a stress-free journey. It helps us to keep proper perspective, stay on the right track and be ourselves.

It was a cloudless, sunny day. Graeme was enjoying the drive. His flight had arrived at 10.00 am, right on time. He'd had an easy time at the car rental company. He was in a relaxed frame of mind as he headed off to his business appointment. It was a wonderful day.

Gradually, Graeme's enjoyment turned to unease and then to anxiety. Something was wrong. He thought back to the moment at the rental car counter when he had turned down the offer of both the map and the GPS. As much as he hated to admit it, he was on the wrong highway.

Living Wholly

Graeme took out his phone and called the rental car company. He found out that his starting point had been wrong. He had taken the wrong turn when he left the rental car office. He freaked out. He was going to be late for his meeting. Suddenly, Graeme didn't feel like that cocksure person who had told the agent behind the counter, "I don't need that. I have a perfect sense of direction and I never get lost." As painful as it was, he had to confess that he'd messed up.

Starting With God

Starting right is important in the shift to living wholly with clarity and peace through honest, surrendered, heart praying. While we can correct as we go along, the journey is much smoother when we start off on the right foot. It is no different with prayer.

Jesus started with God. It's not only that when he gave his disciples what we now know as the Lord's prayer the first phrase was to God: "Our Father." We also see this in his own praying. As we noted earlier in this chapter, Jesus' prayers showed a close relationship with God. Now, let's just look at an example of Jesus starting with God in prayer.

Before Jesus healed Lazarus, he prayed this prayer: "Father, I thank you for having heard me" (John 11:41). As in the Lord's prayer, Jesus started with God, establishing their relationship and the basis on which Jesus was praying to God.

It is a familial relationship. This is not the approach you would give to a distant God. Rather, this is the God who is knowable and relatable. What else does this approach tell us about the God with whom we start? Let's take a look at the parable of the prodigal son to uncover some more about this God with whom we start our praying. You can read the full story that Jesus told in the Gospel of Luke (Luke 15:11–32). Here is what we can conclude about relationship and security from this important story.

When we start our prayers with God in the same vein as Jesus did, we start with a God who does not stand in the way of God' children exercising their choice to stay in or leave God's ways. At the same time, this is a God whose love for the errant child never fails and who notices when this child returns. As a matter of fact, we are praying to a God who will lay aside all decorum and run to meet the prodigal child with love and forgiveness, just happy to see that child return to the fold. This God holds in tension appreciation for the faithful child with celebration and joy for the wayward child who has come home. Why wouldn't you start your prayers with this God? Unless you're like Iris.

Iris liked to get to the heart of the matter. When she prayed, she jumped straight into telling God what she wanted. There were no preliminaries; not even the basic courtesies as when you start a conversation with someone else. Her approach to God was tantamount to going up to someone and saying, "Give me the laptop in your hand." That would be deemed rude and discourteous in real life. There are two aspects to starting our prayers with God.

The first is that prayer is about God. It is to God we pray and as we saw with Jesus and looked at earlier in this chapter, we start with God as loving Father/parent and the security we get from God's posture and actions toward us. We learn this clearly in Jesus' life and the story of the Father and the son who had

Living Wholly

gone astray, popularly knows as The Prodigal Son (Luke 15:11–32). Of course, there is more about God that we need to acknowledge as we saw when we talked about worship earlier in this chapter and touched on in chapter two, "Missing God." Let's look at the other aspect of starting our praying with God.

Starting our prayers with God is a matter of respect. Greet God. Acknowledge God as the one who is over you. At the same time acknowledge God's love and grace to you and communicate with God freely.

Starting with God, therefore, is recognizing God and all that God is. It is surrendering who we are and what we want to God. It is allowing God's will to be done in our lives. It is ensuring that we are not missing prayers. For this to happen, our hearts have to be receptive toward God and our prayers come from our hearts. This leads us to experience God more fully and live with greater clarity and peace.

Dealing with you

Seth looked into the mirror. Did people see the monster that he really was? That's how he thought of himself.

On the outside, Seth looked just fine. On the inside, he was eaten up with a sense of being less than others and guilt over past mistakes that had affected others adversely. This affected everything. Day by day, he just went through the motions never fully engaging with anything or anyone. He was not living wholly.

One day, his friend Leo got him to open up. Seth told him what had happened in the past, how he felt about it, as well as the sense of inferiority he had carried hidden his entire life. Leo listened. Then Leo reminded Seth that he was God's unique creation with singular gifts and a place that no one else could take. Leo reminded Seth of God's forgiveness; that it didn't matter that he wasn't perfect. As a matter of fact, God knew that Seth wasn't perfect. Yet, God loved Seth and offered Seth forgiveness through Jesus Christ. Seth for his turn, listened. In that moment he didn't respond to Leo one way or another.

Later when he was on his own, Seth prayed. He prayed to God based on what Leo had told him about God. He asked God to forgive him not only for what he had done but also for doubting that he was as wonderful and unique as God had said. He felt a release. He began to see the future once again.

Accepting who God says we are is a key part of the journey to living wholly. In our praying we start with God, then we move to receiving what God says about us.

For starters, we must accept and believe Psalm 139:14–15 which states that we are "fearfully and wonderfully made. . . . intricately woven in the depths of the earth." We are wonderful beings and should be awed at God's work in us. This is true of us collectively and it is true of us individually. We bring different gifts. Each of us has a place to fill that is unique to us. Part of our praying should be direction for how and where God would have us be and use these gifts.

Accepting the wonderful way in which we are made brings us face-to-face with God's love—another moment of awe. The Lord of the universe loves us and places a high value on us. It is so high that not only did God make us with care and wonder but sent God's son to die for us. It is a wonderful thing. There are no adequate words to describe it. If God sees us this way, how could we devalue ourselves? How could we talk down to ourselves?

Living Wholly

How dare we allow others to make us less than what God says we are? It's time to release thanksgiving to God for God's love, receive it, and live out of it.

At the same time, we have to guard against an unrealistic view of ourselves. There is a part of us that is broken and needs mending by God.

Isn't it the truth that everybody wants to be considered a good person. It's interesting that Jesus said that only God is good (Luke 18:19). The more I see, the more I am convinced of this. I have seen too many "good" people commit atrocities great and small against others. After all, what is the criteria that we use for good? Is it a well-manicured yard? Is it a certain amount in the bank account? Is it getting to the top of the ladder? What is it? Different people and groups define "good" differently. Here's the thing. At the end of the day, who knows what is in the heart of another human being? Therein lies the crux of the matter.

Realistically then, we all need a change of heart that only God can give. And then, it is a day-by-day, moment-by-moment reliance upon God to continue to change and purify our hearts; to turn us from our inward look to look up to God and out to others; to love up and out with attitudes and deeds that are consistent with our words (1 John 3:18). Accordingly, when we pray let us be honest about who we are and our need for God's mercy, grace, and strength.

When we pray in this way, we are empowered to drive with our focus through the windshield and not the rearview mirror. Dealing with ourselves in the light of who our loving God says we are leaves us free to pull the pieces of our lives together, live joyfully in the present with an eye to the future. Thus, we can be our true selves, open to God's vision and direction.

How to Pray

Praying In a Real Way

God is real. Unless we embrace this reality we will be unable to offer up honest, surrendered, heart praying. The clarity and peace that we seek in this life will be elusive because we have closed the door to knowing God more fully. We will miss the life that's complete and whole. Everything we've discussed in this book so far moves toward this. Yes. God is real. More real than Mila's father.

Mila talked with her father every day. She liked to think that he was there for her. She especially talked to him when she had a problem with her mother. She had lots of those. One was major. Eventually, Mila became stuck. Her father was not responding. As she got older and life became more complex she needed guidance. She just was not getting it from her father.

You see, Mila's father was dead. He had died when she was very small. She still remembered him as being kind and patient with her. She felt that if he had still been alive her life would have been different. Her mother would have been different.

Mila was trapped. She was trapped in her childhood memories of her father. Her conversations with him kept her locked in that stage, unable to adequately deal with her realities, who she was, and who she was becoming. She started to shut down. She would not go anywhere or do anything. Although Mila knew about God, her deceased father was more real to her. Yet, her father could not do anything for her.

Fortunately, Mila got help to uncover and examine her past and face her current reality. She was led to encounter the true and living God. With God's help she started to move on. She

Living Wholly

resumed her educational endeavors as she gained clarity and peace.

When God is not real to us, we go in so many different directions, looking for help, seeking to fill the void. While there are many worthwhile support systems and programs, God is the one who fills us at the deepest level and gives us a peace that defies logic. Even when the world seems to be crashing down on us, we have this peace. If we look closely, we'll find that when we are missing this peace and clarity God has stopped being real to us. Why?

When God is not real to us, we are not real with God. Our prayers are not real and genuine. Thus, we are missing the real God and as we saw in chapter two, "Missing God," we give homage to and seek to manipulate our conception of God. However, we need to seek to know God increasingly on God's terms and push on to do so.

As we press on to know God, we come to God as real people with full disclosure and candor. Now, this does not mean that we come as perfect people. We're not. As we said earlier, as Jesus said, only God is good. Therefore, we come as we are for God to change us. We come without holding on to our insecurities and trophies. Some of these trophies are negative behaviors that impact others adversely of which we say, "That's just who I am." No. To pray in a real way is to bring these anxieties and prizes and lay them at the foot of the cross. It is to stop missing ourselves as we get real with God. In addition, it is to be open and allow the transforming work of the Spirit in our lives. That's also what surrender is about.

Therefore, in our real praying as real people praying to a real God we enter a real relationship that is two-way. We don't journey on a one-way street. Rather, we are constantly open to hearing what the Spirit would say to us. Then we go and do as God says.

However, be aware of this danger. We are not perfected in this life, thus we face the risk of going off on a tangent, doing our own thing and saying that it is of God. How do we avoid this pitfall? We avoid it by being grounded in the Word of God and involved in the community of faith. Don't be a lone ranger as you pray in a real way.

Conclusion

Clarity and peace in a changing and often tumultuous world are attainable. They can be yours. They come out of experiencing God more fully. All it takes is for you to recognize who you are, understand your need of God, get a vision of God and God's reign, then let go of the reins of your life and go to God with honest, surrendered, heart praying. Then you will live wholly for none of the ingredients of the cake of your life will be missing.

This is our prayer for you at *SurrenderInPrayer*. This is why the author of this book and the resources of this ministry are available to you. God bless you.

What's Next?

If this book has blessed you in any way, please be a blessing in return. Would you leave a review where you bought this book? As simple as it may seem, your review will help us to reach more people.

We would love to welcome you into the SurrenderInPrayer community. Join now to receive our weekly blog post, monthly newsletter, and inspirational updates in your inbox: http://surrenderinprayer.com/join.

Be sure to get the rest of the *How to Pray* suite to enhance your intimate connection with God.

Thank you for sharing the journey with us.

***How to Pray: Living Wholly Through Honest,
Surrendered, Heart Praying***

The Book
The Study Guide
The Devotional
The CD

www.ingramcontent.com/pod-product-compliance
Lightning Source LLC
Chambersburg PA
CBHW071155090426
42736CB00012B/2338